The Little Norsky's Coloring & Activity Book

NORSELAND PRESS

Draw a picture of something you'd like to see or do in Norway.

Bryggen
"brig-en"

Have you ever seen a picture of rows of very colorful old buildings next to a harbor? In Bergen, one of Norway's biggest cities, there are just such buildings, all lined up next to the city's harbor. These buildings, called *bryggen* in Norwegian, were built over 500 years ago by a trading organization we call the Hanseatic League.

The Hanseatic League buildings in Bergen are painted in shades of red, orange, and white. What colors would you like to use?

Four In A Row

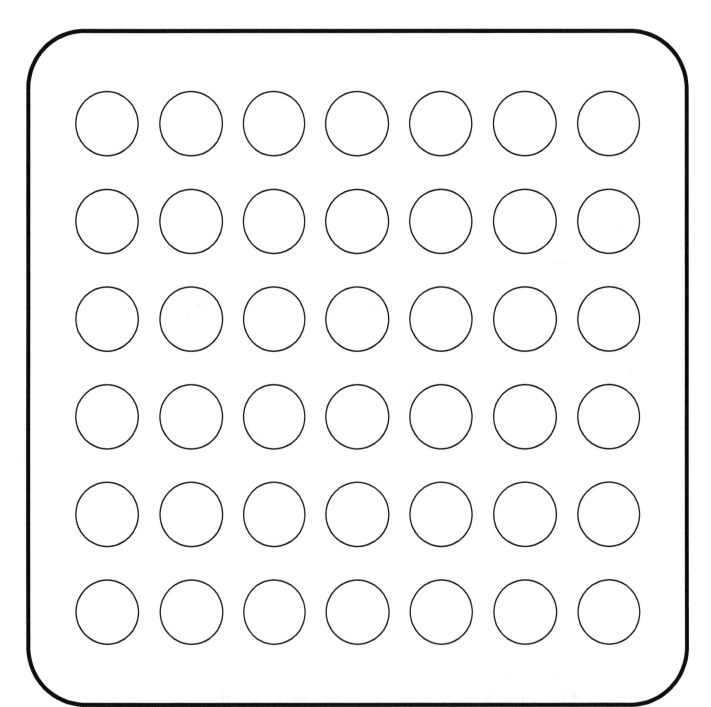

Count to four in Norwegian while you play this classic game.

EN (ehn)   *TO* (too)   *TRE* (tray)   *FIRE* (fee-reh)

Galgespill
"GAHL - ge - speel"

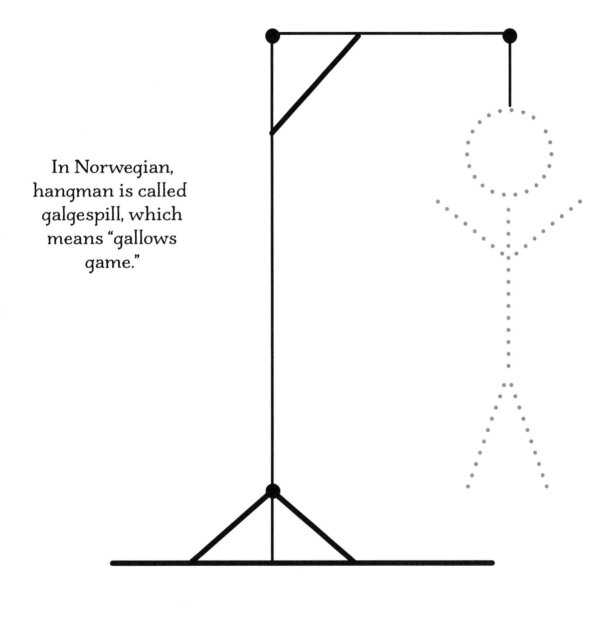

In Norwegian, hangman is called galgespill, which means "gallows game."

A B C D E F G H I J K L M N
O P Q R S T U V W X Y Z

Bondesjakk
"BAHN deh shahk"

Play some games of bondesjakk, which translates to "farmer's chess."

Bondesjakk
"BAHN deh shahk"

Play some games of bondesjakk, which translates to "farmer's chess."

Sekskantspill
"SEKS-skant speel"

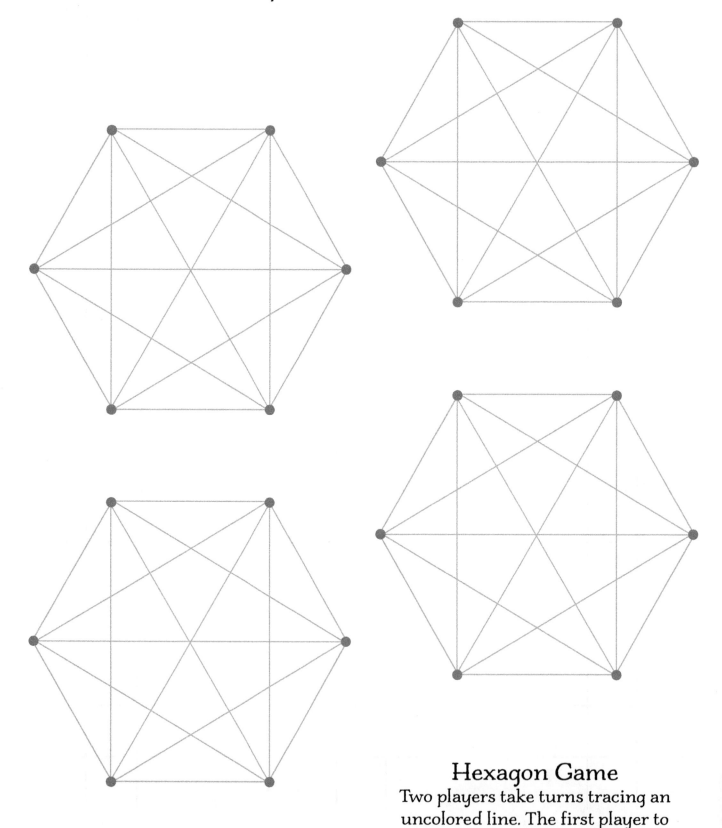

Hexagon Game
Two players take turns tracing an uncolored line. The first player to create a triangle loses the game.

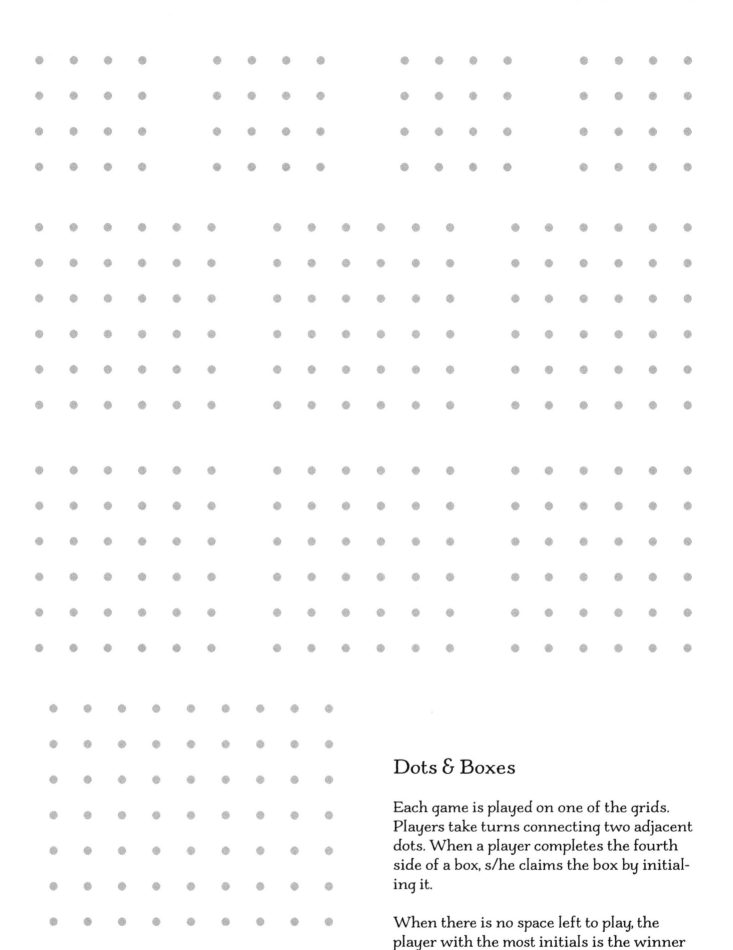

Dots & Boxes

Each game is played on one of the grids. Players take turns connecting two adjacent dots. When a player completes the fourth side of a box, s/he claims the box by initialing it.

When there is no space left to play, the player with the most initials is the winner of that game.

Draw your own cartoon strip set in Norway.

Mosaikk
"moo- SAKE"

Create a mosaic design.

Draw a picture of something you'd like to see or do in Norway.

Vikingskip
"VEE-king sheep"

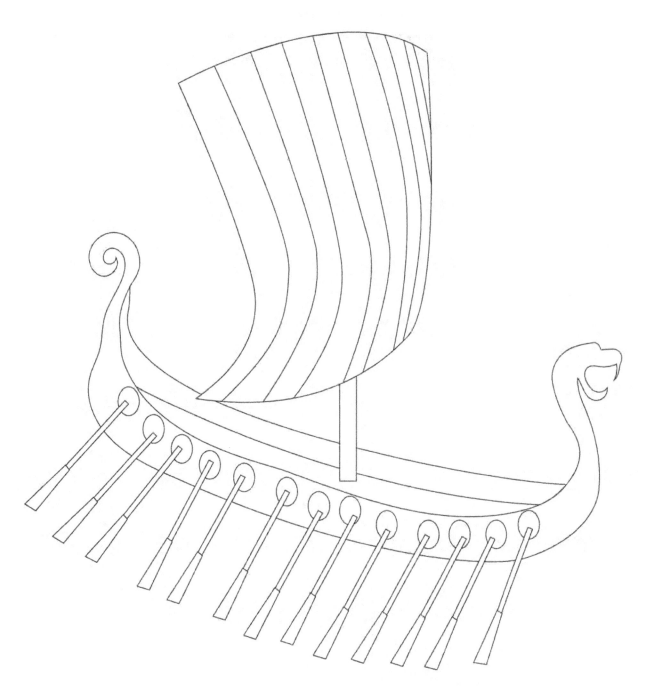

The vikings lived over 900 years ago, but people today are as interested as ever in these seafaring warriors. Viking longships, such as the simplified version shown here, used both people power (rowers) and wind power (via the sail) to reach speeds of up to 17 knots (about 19 miles per hour). Longships were double-ended, as you can see in this illustration. Can you think of any reasons why being able to go backward and forward, without turning the ship around, would give the vikings an advantage?

Four In A Row

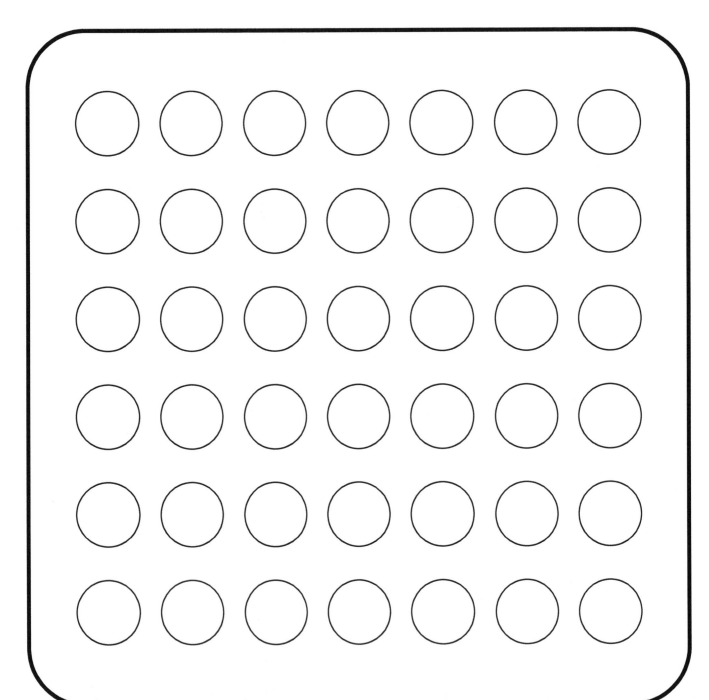

Count to four in Norwegian while you play this classic game.

EN (ehn)   *TO* (too)   *TRE* (tray)   *FIRE* (fee-reh)

Galgespill
"GAHL - ge - speel"

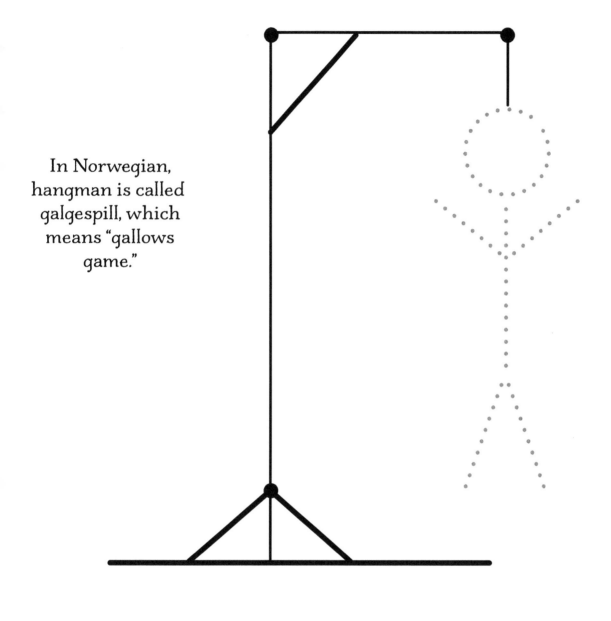

In Norwegian, hangman is called galgespill, which means "gallows game."

A B C D E F G H I J K L M N
O P Q R S T U V W X Y Z

Bondesjakk
"BAHN deh shahk"

Play some games of bondesjakk, which translates to "farmer's chess."

Bondesjakk

"BAHN deh shahk"

Play some games of bondesjakk, which translates to "farmer's chess."

Sekskantspill
"SEKS-skant speel"

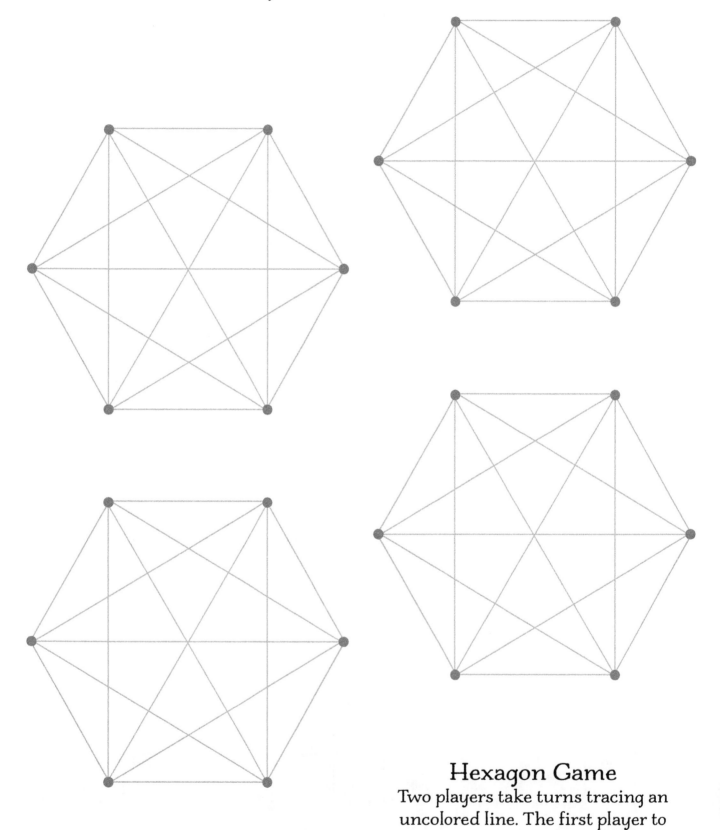

Hexagon Game
Two players take turns tracing an uncolored line. The first player to create a triangle loses the game.

Dots & Boxes

Each game is played on one of the grids. Players take turns connecting two adjacent dots. When a player completes the fourth side of a box, s/he claims the box by initialing it.

When there is no space left to play, the player with the most initials is the winner of that game.

Mosaikk
"moo- SAKE"

Create a mosaic design.

Draw a picture of something you'd like to see or do in Norway.

Stavkirken
"stav - sheer - ken"

Stave churches (Stavkirken in Norwegian) were built in northwestern Europe during medieval times, about the year 1150. Today, the vast majority of surviving stave churches are located in Norway.

Four In A Row

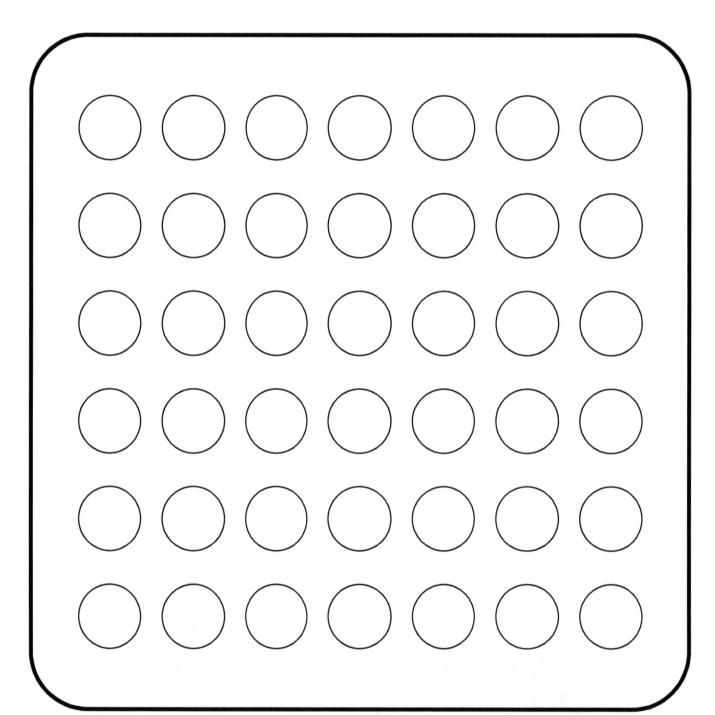

Count to four in Norwegian while you play this classic game.

EN (ehn)   *TO* (too)   *TRE* (tray)   *FIRE* (fee-reh)

Galgespill
"GAHL - ge - speel"

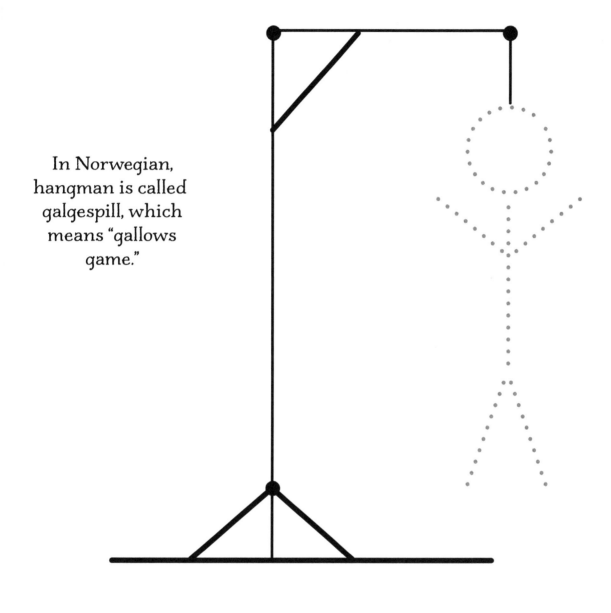

In Norwegian, hangman is called galgespill, which means "gallows game."

A B C D E F G H I J K L M N
O P Q R S T U V W X Y Z

Bondesjakk

"BAHN deh shahk"

Play some games of bondesjakk, which translates to "farmer's chess."

Bondesjakk
"BAHN deh shahk"

Play some games of bondesjakk, which translates to "farmer's chess."

Sekskantspill
"SEKS-skant speel"

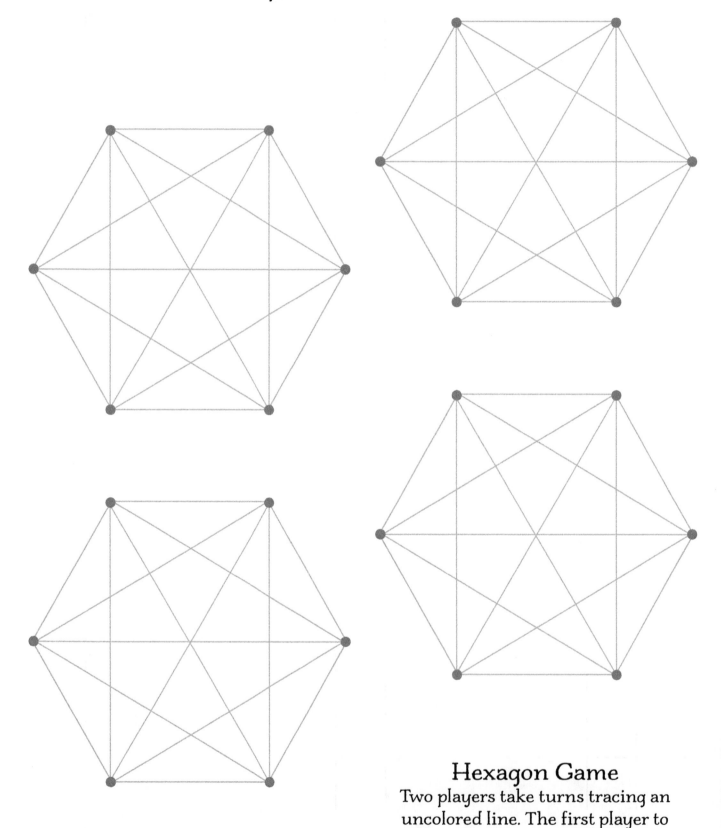

Hexagon Game
Two players take turns tracing an uncolored line. The first player to create a triangle loses the game.

Dots & Boxes

Each game is played on one of the grids. Players take turns connecting two adjacent dots. When a player completes the fourth side of a box, s/he claims the box by initialing it.

When there is no space left to play, the player with the most initials is the winner of that game.

Draw your own cartoon strip set in Norway.

Mosaikk
"moo- SAKE"

Create a mosaic design.

Draw a picture of something you'd like to see or do in Norway.

Langrenn

"LAHN-grenn"

The sport that we call cross country skiing, or Nordic skiing, is very popular in Norway. Hundreds of years ago, skiing was a necessary means of transportation for hunting, gathering firewood, and simply getting from one farm or village to another. Today, skiing is an activity that Norwegians of all ages enjoy, with children learning how to ski almost as soon as they can walk.

Four In A Row

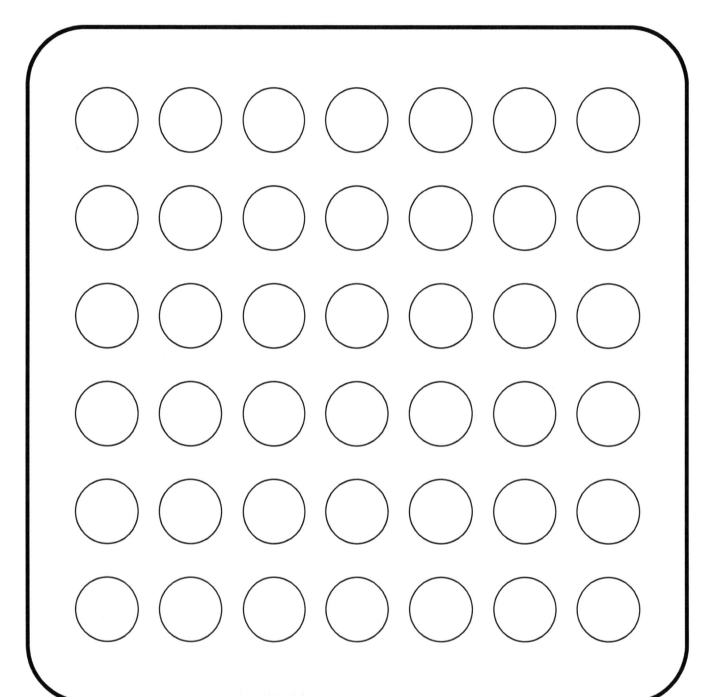

Count to four in Norwegian while you play this classic game.

EN (ehn)   *TO* (too)   *TRE* (tray)   *FIRE* (fee-reh)

Galgespill
"GAHL - ge - speel"

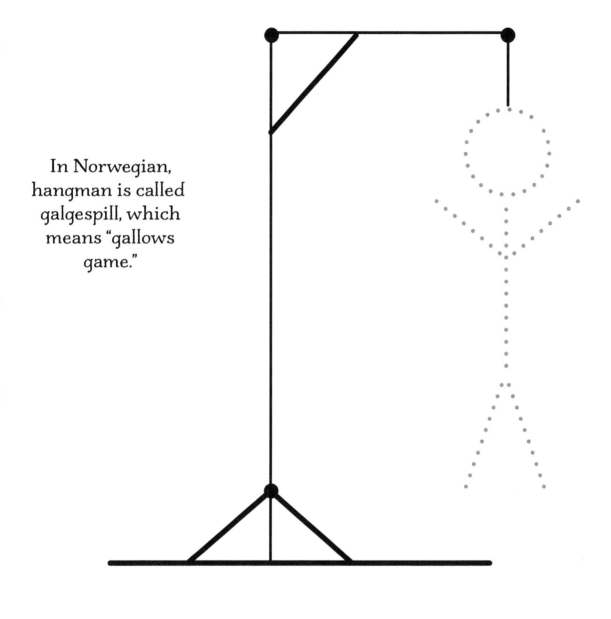

In Norwegian, hangman is called galgespill, which means "gallows game."

A B C D E F G H I J K L M N
O P Q R S T U V W X Y Z

Bondesjakk
"BAHN deh shahk"

Play some games of bondesjakk, which translates to "farmer's chess."

Bondesjakk
"BAHN deh shahk"

Play some games of bondesjakk, which translates to "farmer's chess."

Sekskantspill
"SEKS-skant speel"

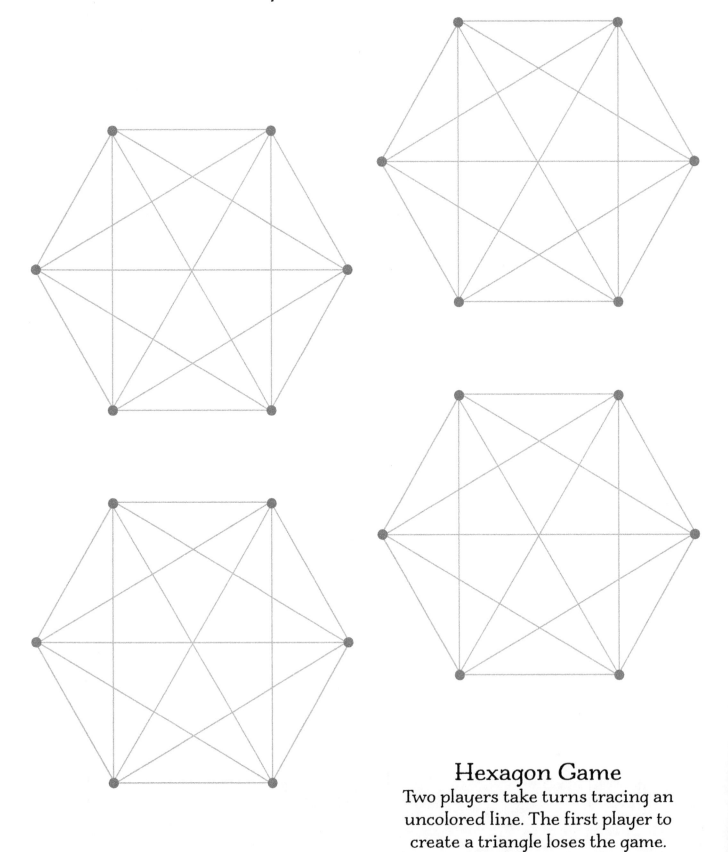

Hexagon Game
Two players take turns tracing an uncolored line. The first player to create a triangle loses the game.

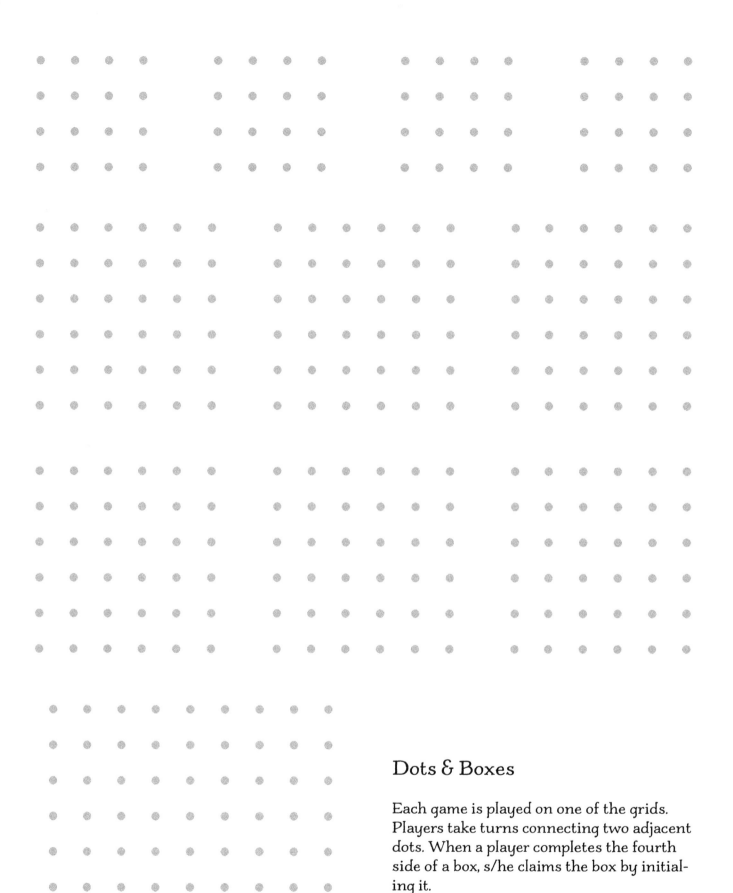

Dots & Boxes

Each game is played on one of the grids. Players take turns connecting two adjacent dots. When a player completes the fourth side of a box, s/he claims the box by initialing it.

When there is no space left to play, the player with the most initials is the winner of that game.

Draw your own cartoon strip set in Norway.

Mosaikk
"moo- SAKE"

Create a mosaic design.

Draw a picture of something you'd like to see or do in Norway.

Skihopping
"SHE - hopping"

Did you know that ski jumping (*skihopping*) has its beginnings in Norway? The world's first ski jump competition took place in the year 1866 in Ofte, Norway. Since that time, ski equipment, apparel, and technique have changed a lot. Ski jumpers today wear colorful suits that are extremely smooth, which helps them fly through the air faster and farther.

Four In A Row

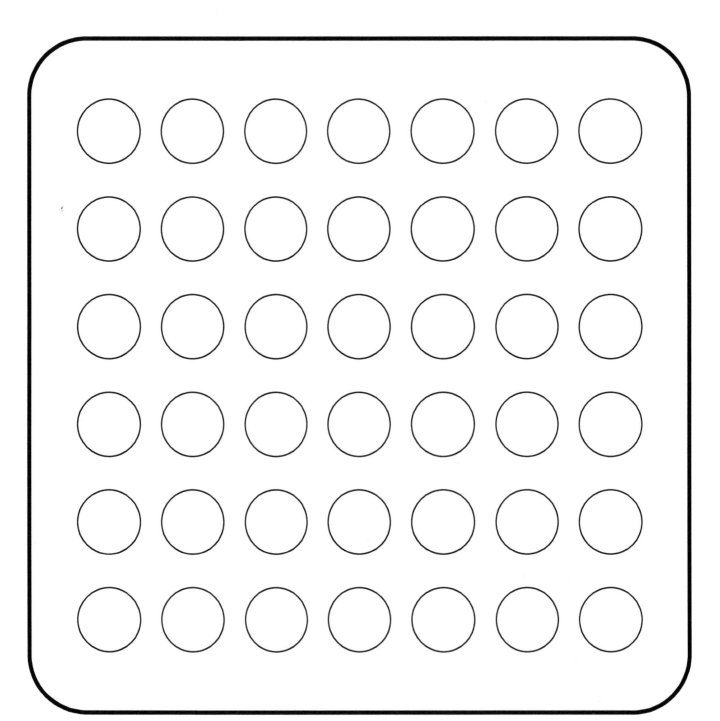

Count to four in Norwegian while you play this classic game.

EN (ehn)   *TO* (too)   *TRE* (tray)   *FIRE* (fee-reh)

Galgespill
"GAHL - ge - speel"

In Norwegian, hangman is called galgespill, which means "gallows game."

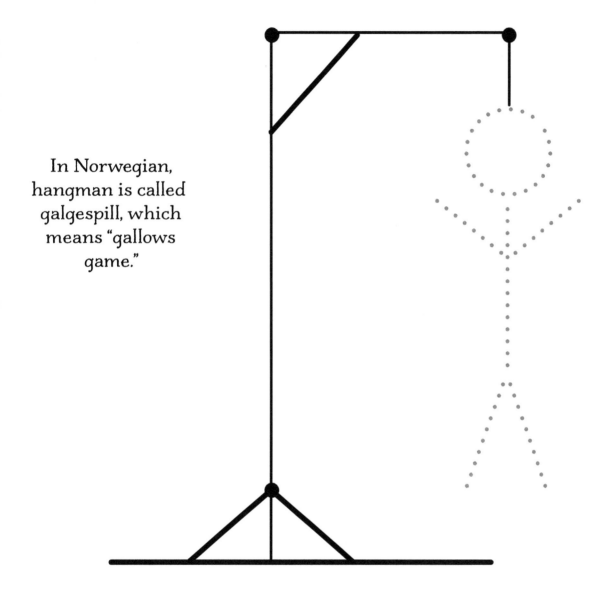

A B C D E F G H I J K L M N
O P Q R S T U V W X Y Z

Bondesjakk
"BAHN deh shahk"

Play some games of bondesjakk, which translates to "farmer's chess."

Bondesjakk
"BAHN deh shahk"

Play some games of bondesjakk, which translates to "farmer's chess."

Sekskantspill
"SEKS-skant speel"

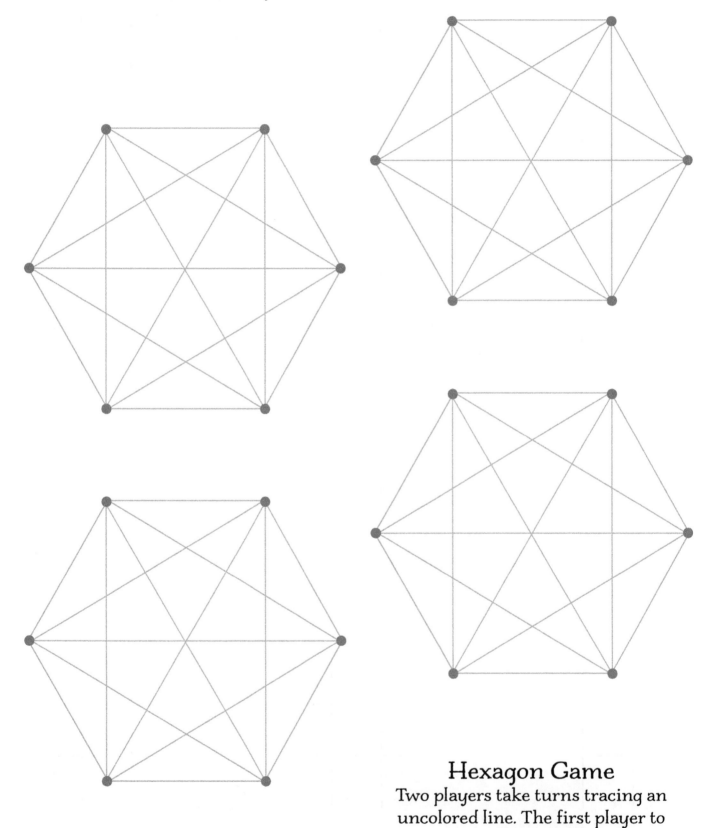

Hexagon Game
Two players take turns tracing an uncolored line. The first player to create a triangle loses the game.

Dots & Boxes

Each game is played on one of the grids. Players take turns connecting two adjacent dots. When a player completes the fourth side of a box, s/he claims the box by initialing it.

When there is no space left to play, the player with the most initials is the winner of that game.

Draw your own cartoon strip set in Norway.

Mosaikk
"moo- SAKE"

Create a mosaic design.

Draw a picture of something you'd like to see or do in Norway.

The Scream is a very famous painting by Norwegian artist Edvard Munch. He created this painting in 1893. The painting, called Skrik in Norwegian, is kept in the National Gallery and Munch Museum in Oslo, Norway.

Four In A Row

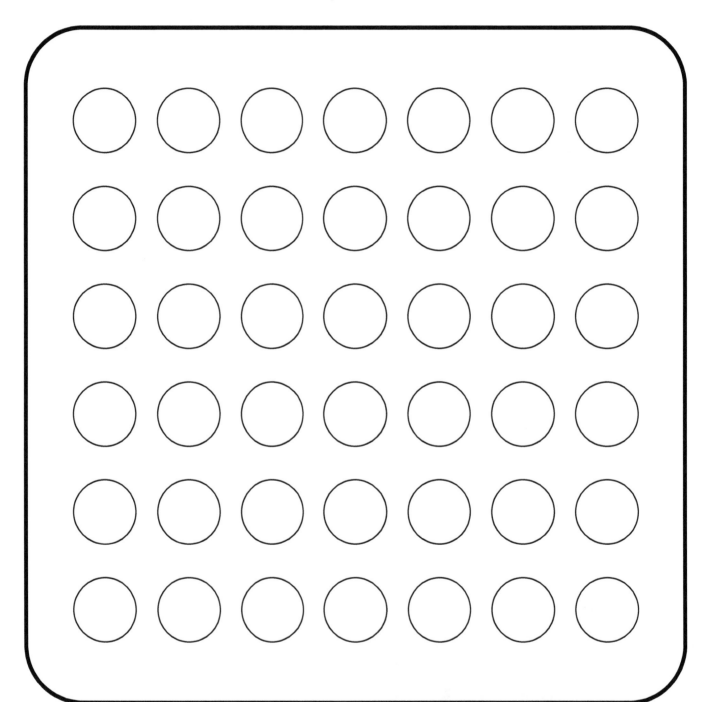

Count to four in Norwegian while you play this classic game.

EN (ehn)   **TO** (too)   **TRE** (tray)   **FIRE** (fee-reh)

Galgespill
"GAHL - ge - speel"

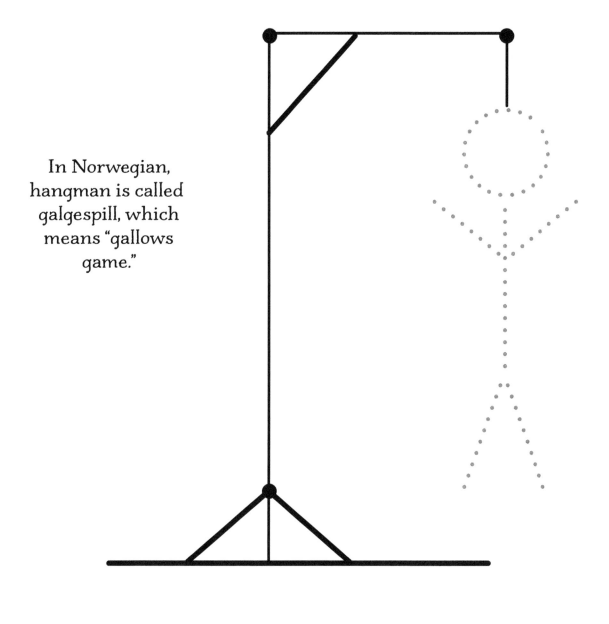

In Norwegian, hangman is called galgespill, which means "gallows game."

A B C D E F G H I J K L M N
O P Q R S T U V W X Y Z

Bondesjakk
"BAHN deh shahk"

Play some games of bondesjakk, which translates to "farmer's chess."

Bondesjakk
"BAHN deh shahk"

Play some games of bondesjakk, which translates to "farmer's chess."

Sekskantspill
"SEKS-skant speel"

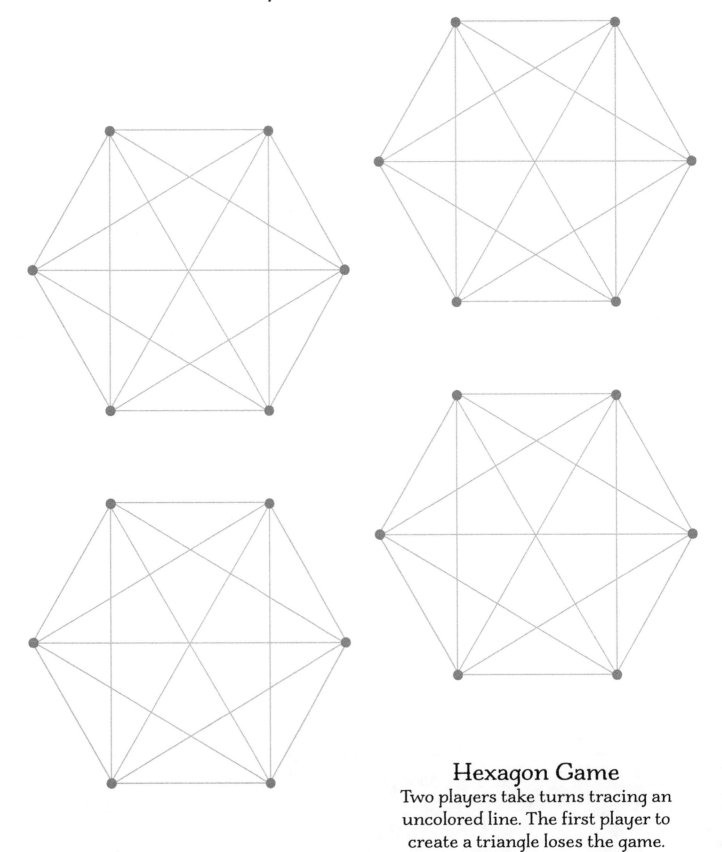

Hexagon Game
Two players take turns tracing an uncolored line. The first player to create a triangle loses the game.

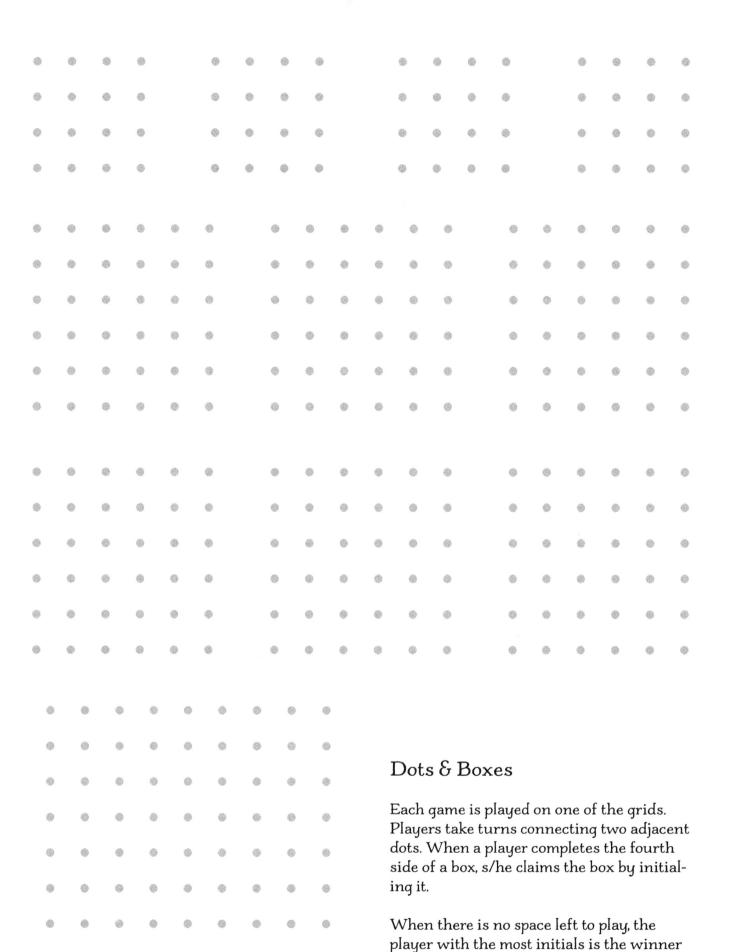

Dots & Boxes

Each game is played on one of the grids. Players take turns connecting two adjacent dots. When a player completes the fourth side of a box, s/he claims the box by initialing it.

When there is no space left to play, the player with the most initials is the winner of that game.

Draw your own cartoon strip set in Norway.

Mosaikk
"moo- SAKE"

Create a mosaic design.

Draw a picture of something you'd like to see or do in Norway.

Fyrtårn
"fear torn"

Lighthouses are very important in Norway due to the massive amount of coastline. The oldest lighthouse (*fyrtårn*) in Norway opened in the year 1655.

Four In A Row

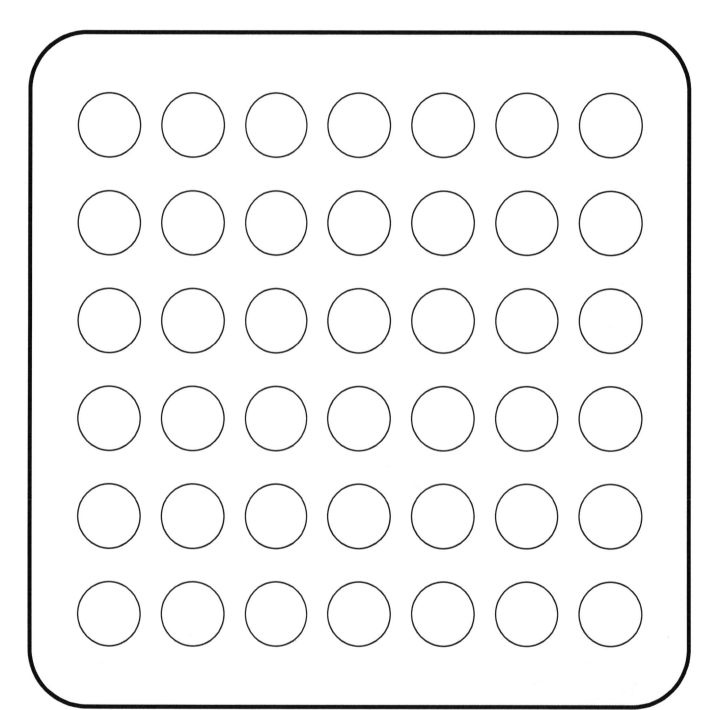

Count to four in Norwegian while you play this classic game.

EN (ehn)   **TO** (too)   **TRE** (tray)   **FIRE** (fee-reh)

Galgespill
"GAHL - ge - speel"

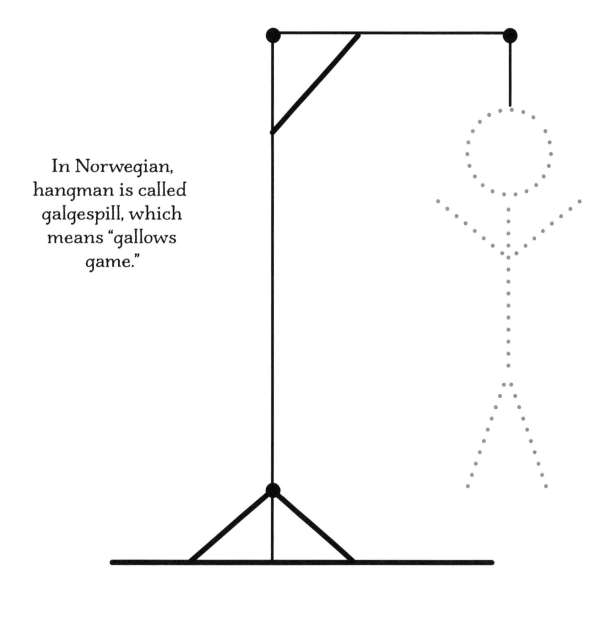

In Norwegian, hangman is called galgespill, which means "gallows game."

_ _ _ _ _ _ _ _ _ _ _ _ _ _

_ _ _ _ _ _ _ _ _ _ _ _ _ _

A B C D E F G H I J K L M N
O P Q R S T U V W X Y Z

Bondesjakk
"BAHN deh shahk"

Play some games of bondesjakk, which translates to "farmer's chess."

Bondesjakk
"BAHN deh shahk"

Play some games of bondesjakk, which translates to "farmer's chess."

Sekskantspill
"SEKS-skant speel"

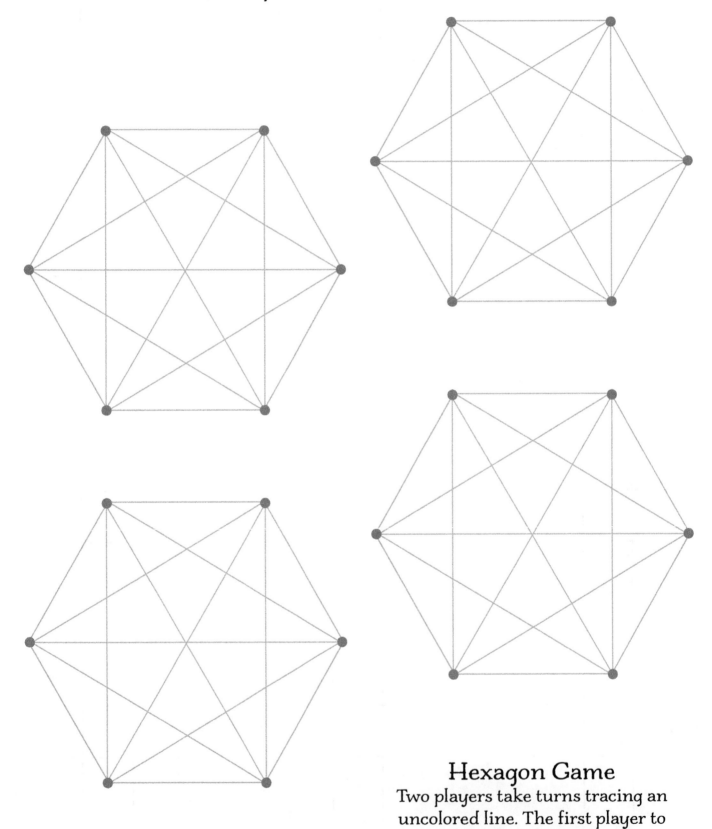

Hexagon Game
Two players take turns tracing an uncolored line. The first player to create a triangle loses the game.

Dots & Boxes

Each game is played on one of the grids. Players take turns connecting two adjacent dots. When a player completes the fourth side of a box, s/he claims the box by initialing it.

When there is no space left to play, the player with the most initials is the winner of that game.

Draw your own cartoon strip set in Norway.

Mosaikk
"moo- SAKE"

Create a mosaic design.

Draw a picture of something you'd like to see or do in Norway.

Frigjøringsdagen

"free yur-ings dahg-en"

For five years during World War II, Norway was occupied by Nazi Germany forces. During this time, Norwegian citizens did not have their normal freedoms. It was a scary time.
On May 8, 1945, Nazi Germany forces withdrew from Norway. This day is remembered as Frigjøringsdagen (Liberation Day) in Norway.

Four In A Row

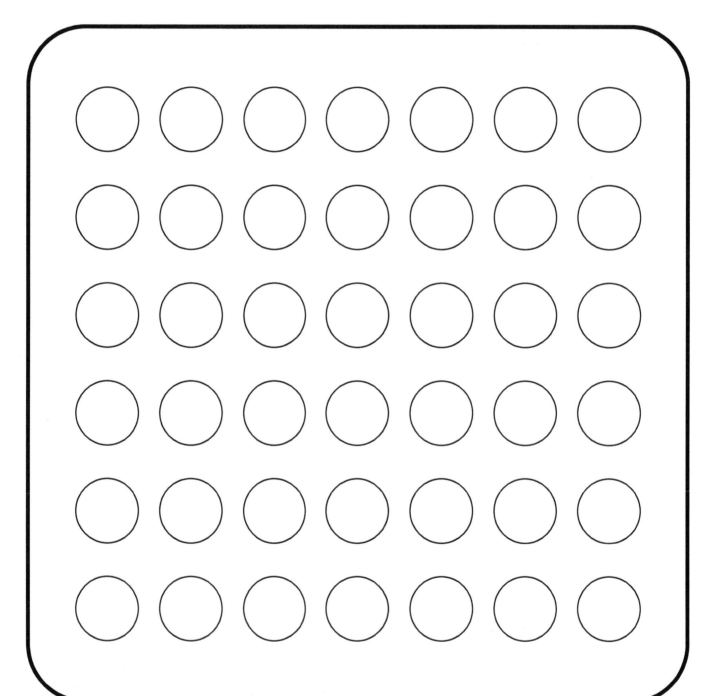

Count to four in Norwegian while you play this classic game.

EN (ehn)   *TO* (too)   *TRE* (tray)   *FIRE* (fee-reh)

Galgespill
"GAHL - ge - speel"

In Norwegian, hangman is called galgespill, which means "gallows game."

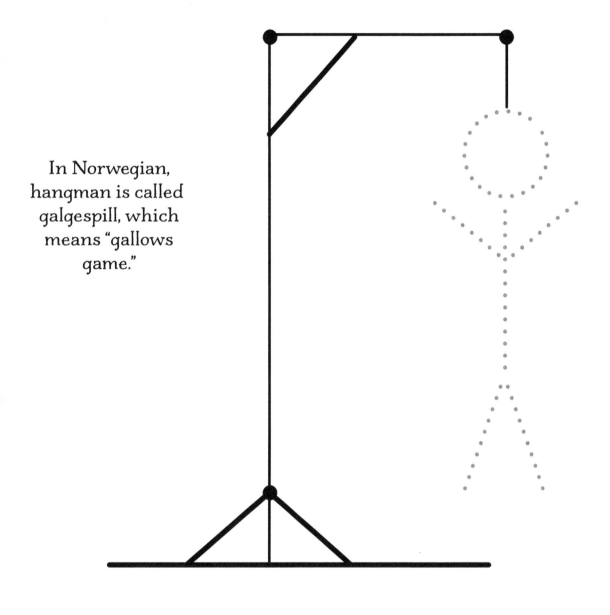

A B C D E F G H I J K L M N
O P Q R S T U V W X Y Z

Bondesjakk

"BAHN deh shahk"

Play some games of bondesjakk, which translates to "farmer's chess."

Bondesjakk
"BAHN deh shahk"

Play some games of bondesjakk, which translates to "farmer's chess."

Sekskantspill
"SEKS-skant speel"

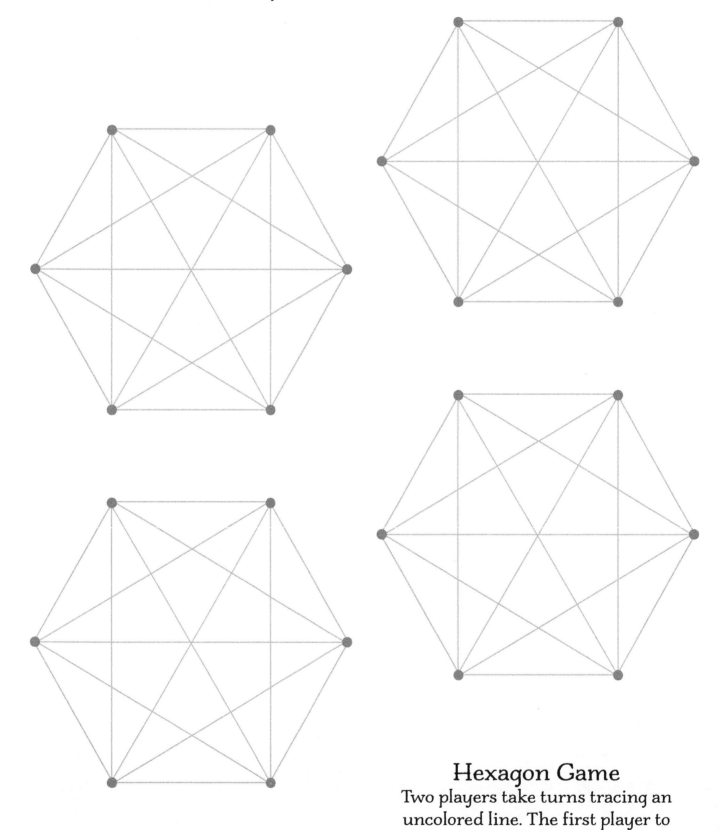

Hexagon Game
Two players take turns tracing an uncolored line. The first player to create a triangle loses the game.

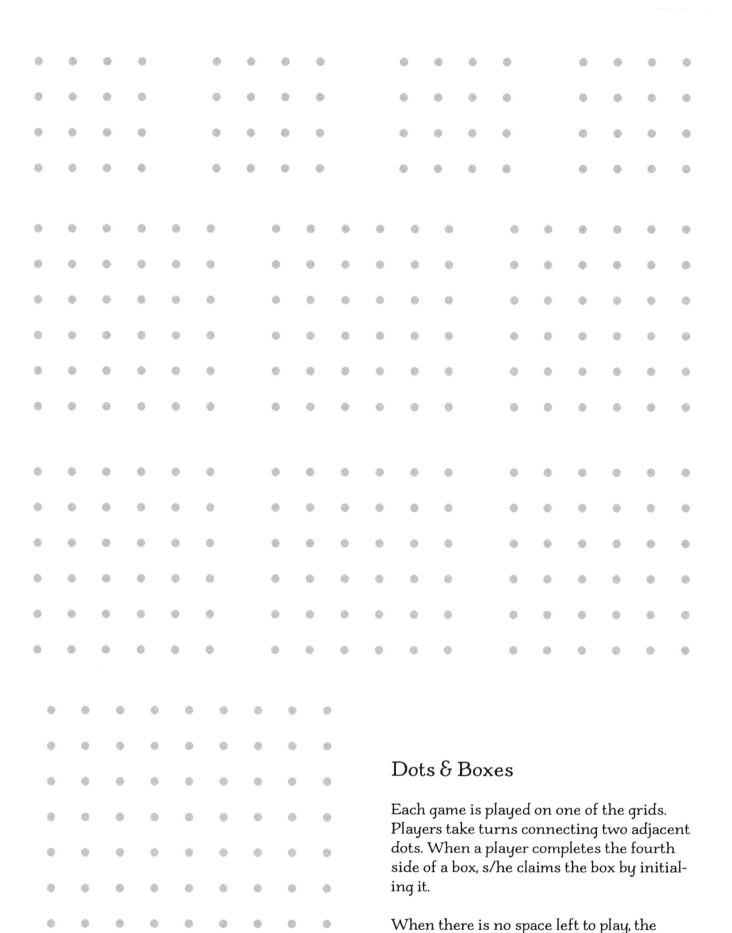

Dots & Boxes

Each game is played on one of the grids. Players take turns connecting two adjacent dots. When a player completes the fourth side of a box, s/he claims the box by initialing it.

When there is no space left to play, the player with the most initials is the winner of that game.

Draw your own cartoon strip set in Norway.

Mosaikk
"moo-SAKE"

Create a mosaic design.

Draw a picture of something you'd like to see or do in Norway.

Norwegian folk art often included animals in addition to flower motifs and geometric shapes. What kinds of animals do you think people would have seen in their everyday lives?

Four In A Row

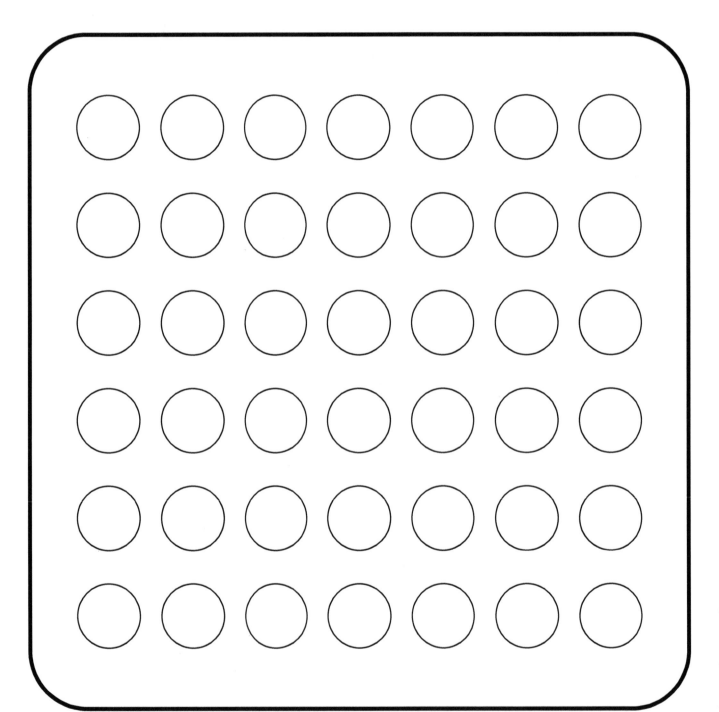

Count to four in Norwegian while you play this classic game.

EN (ehn) **TO** (too) **TRE** (tray) **FIRE** (fee-reh)

Galgespill
"GAHL - ge - speel"

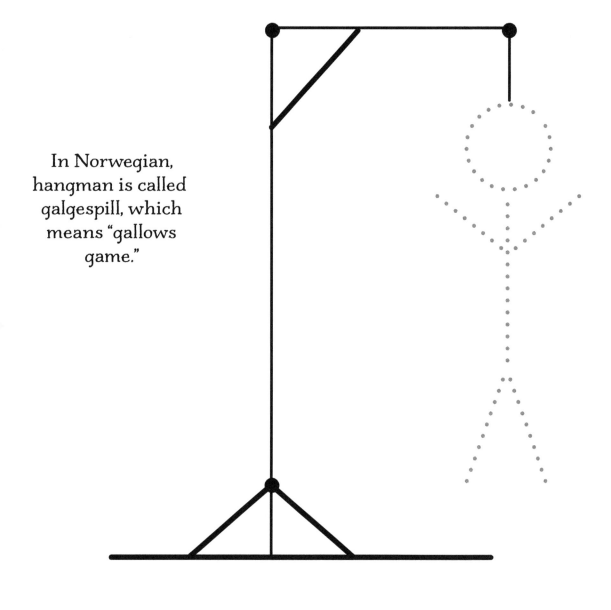

In Norwegian, hangman is called galgespill, which means "gallows game."

A B C D E F G H I J K L M N
O P Q R S T U V W X Y Z

Bondesjakk
"BAHN deh shahk"

Play some games of bondesjakk, which translates to "farmer's chess."

Bondesjakk
"BAHN deh shahk"

Play some games of bondesjakk, which translates to "farmer's chess."

Sekskantspill
"SEKS-skant speel"

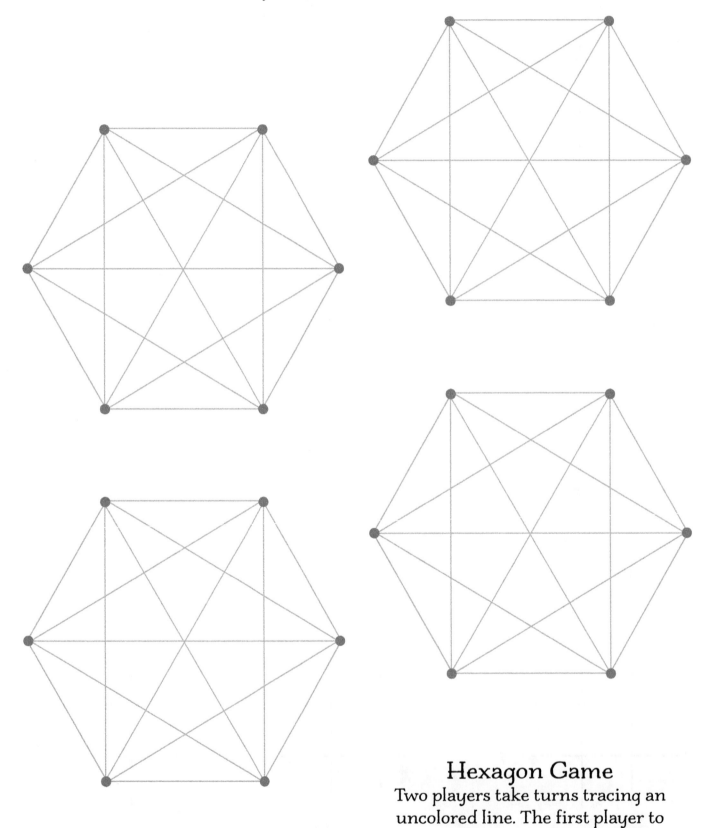

Hexagon Game
Two players take turns tracing an uncolored line. The first player to create a triangle loses the game.

Dots & Boxes

Each game is played on one of the grids. Players take turns connecting two adjacent dots. When a player completes the fourth side of a box, s/he claims the box by initialing it.

When there is no space left to play, the player with the most initials is the winner of that game.

Draw your own cartoon strip set in Norway.

Mosaikk
"moo- SAKE"

Create a mosaic design.

Draw a picture of something you'd like to see or do in Norway.

Folk art is an important part of Norwegian culture. While you color this folk-art-styled design, think about what it would have been like to learn this artistic skill hundreds of years ago.

Four In A Row

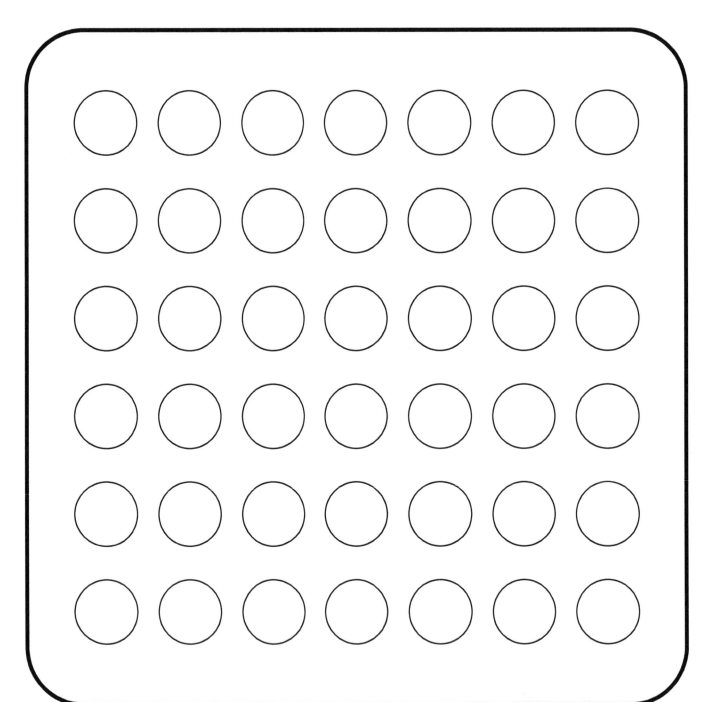

Count to four in Norwegian while you play this classic game.

EN (ehn)   **TO** (too)   **TRE** (tray)   **FIRE** (fee-reh)

Galgespill
"GAHL - ge - speel"

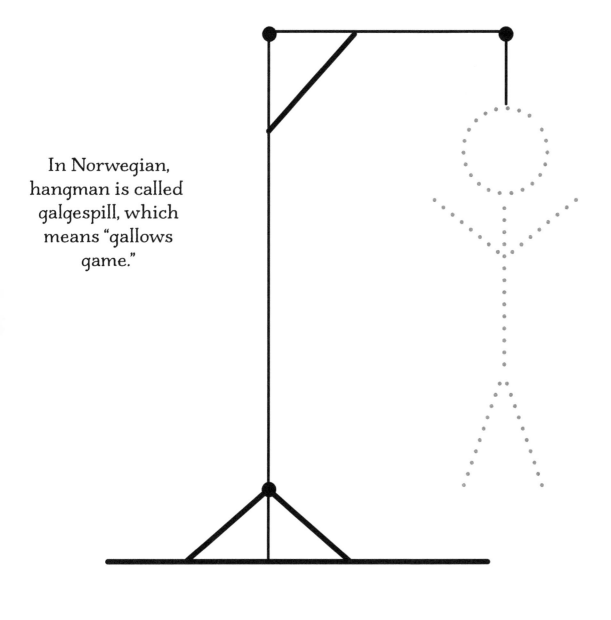

In Norwegian, hangman is called galgespill, which means "gallows game."

A B C D E F G H I J K L M N
O P Q R S T U V W X Y Z

Sekskantspill
"SEKS-skant speel"

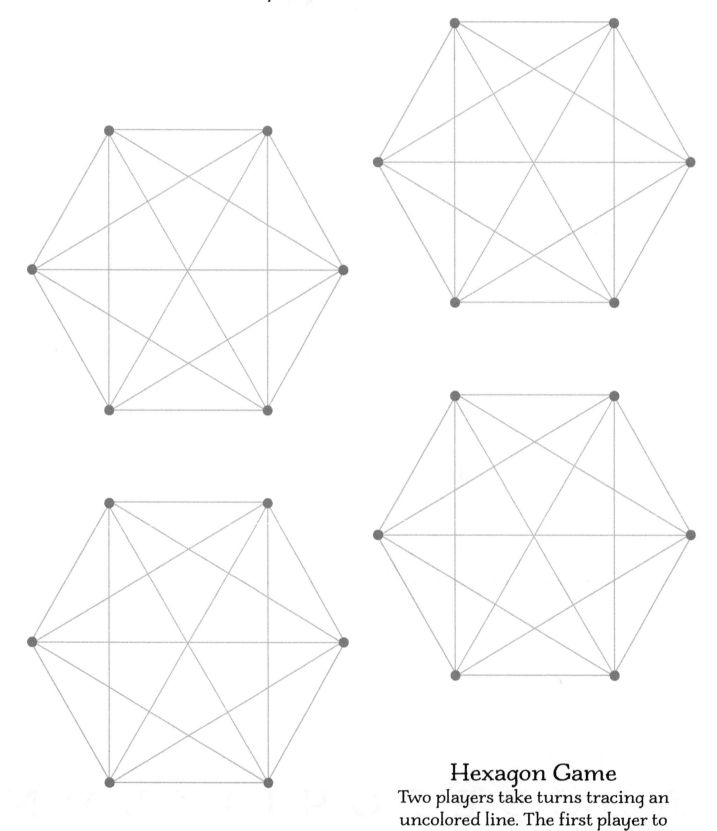

Hexagon Game
Two players take turns tracing an uncolored line. The first player to create a triangle loses the game.

Dots & Boxes

Each game is played on one of the grids. Players take turns connecting two adjacent dots. When a player completes the fourth side of a box, s/he claims the box by initialing it.

When there is no space left to play, the player with the most initials is the winner of that game.

Draw your own cartoon strip set in Norway.

Mosaikk
"moo- SAKE"

Create a mosaic design.

Draw a picture of something you'd like to see or do in Norway.

Printed in the USA
CPSIA information can be obtained
at www.ICGtesting.com
LVHW061001220823
755950LV00020B/229